D1716897

DOLPHINS SET II

ATLANTIC HUMPBACKED DOLPHINS

Kristin Petrie
ABDO Publishing Company

visit us at
www.abdopub.com

Published by ABDO Publishing Company, 4940 Viking Drive, Edina, Minnesota 55435.
Copyright © 2006 by Abdo Consulting Group, Inc. International copyrights reserved in all
countries. No part of this book may be reproduced in any form without written permission from
the publisher. The Checkerboard Library™ is a trademark and logo of ABDO Publishing
Company.

Printed in the United States.

Cover Photo: Graeme Hornby
Interior Photos: © Amos Nachoum / SeaPics.com p. 13; © Doug Perrine / SeaPics.com pp. 14,
     15, 21; Graeme Hornby p. 5; Richard Parnell p. 10; Tim Collins pp. 7, 12, 17, 19; Uko
     Gorter pp. 6-7

Series Coordinator: Megan M. Gunderson
Editors: Megan M. Gunderson, Megan Murphy
Art Direction, Diagram, & Map: Neil Klinepier

Library of Congress Cataloging-in-Publication Data

Petrie, Kristin, 1970-
     Atlantic humpbacked dolphins / Kristin Petrie.
          p. cm. -- (Dolphins. Set II)
     Includes index.
     ISBN 1-59679-300-7
      1. Atlantic humpbacked dolphin--Juvenile literature. I. Title.

QL737.C432P465 2005
599.53--dc22

                                                                    2005045798

CONTENTS

ATLANTIC HUMPBACKED DOLPHINS

If you have ever been to a zoo, you may have seen dolphins there. These fun creatures were probably common bottlenose dolphins. Like other ocean dolphins, these **cetaceans** belong to the Delphinidae **family**.

Some dolphin species are found all over the world. But, others are not as common and may be found only in one small area. Some live in the ocean. And, some live only in rivers. Dolphins can be many different sizes and colors.

One species of dolphin is the *Sousa teuszii*. It is more commonly known as the Atlantic humpbacked dolphin. This dolphin's name reveals that they live in the Atlantic Ocean. And, it gives you a hint about what they look like!

Atlantic humpbacked dolphins can look very similar to common bottlenose dolphins. However, their hump becomes more prominent as they age. So, the two species become easier to tell apart.

SIZE, SHAPE, AND COLOR

The Atlantic humpbacked dolphin has a robust body.
It has a large **melon**, a long snout, and rounded chest
flippers. This dolphin also has a hump on which its
dorsal fin rests. A second smaller hump is found near
the **flukes**.

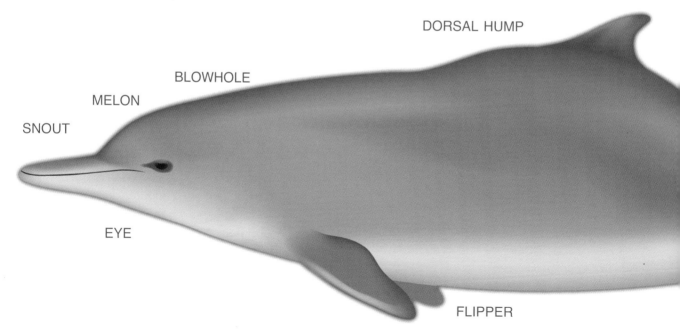

DORSAL HUMP

BLOWHOLE

MELON

SNOUT

EYE

FLIPPER

The color of
Atlantic
humpbacked
dolphins varies
from light to dark
gray. Their color
may change as

Like many other species in the Delphinidae family, Atlantic humpbacked dolphins have one blowhole on the top of the head as well as a notch in the flukes.

they age. They may be speckled with lighter gray or white markings. And like most other dolphins, the belly is a lighter color than the rest of the body.

Atlantic humpbacked dolphins are about three feet (1 m) long at birth. By the time they are adults, they are at least double this length. The adult dolphin is 72 to 96 inches (183 to 244 cm) long. Its weight ranges between 220 and 330 pounds (100 and 150 kg)!

FLUKE

WHERE THEY LIVE

Atlantic humpbacked dolphins live in the warm, tropical waters off the coast of West Africa. They are a common sight from Mauritania to Cameroon, and as far south as Angola. They are generally found in waters warmer than 60 degrees Fahrenheit (16°C).

These dolphins also prefer shallow water that is less than 70 feet (20 m) deep. And, they don't usually venture too far from shore. They are even known to swim into estuaries, where rivers meet the sea.

Some scientists believe these dolphins **migrate**. But, scientists have not studied this species as closely as others. So, there is still much to be learned about Atlantic humpbacked dolphins.

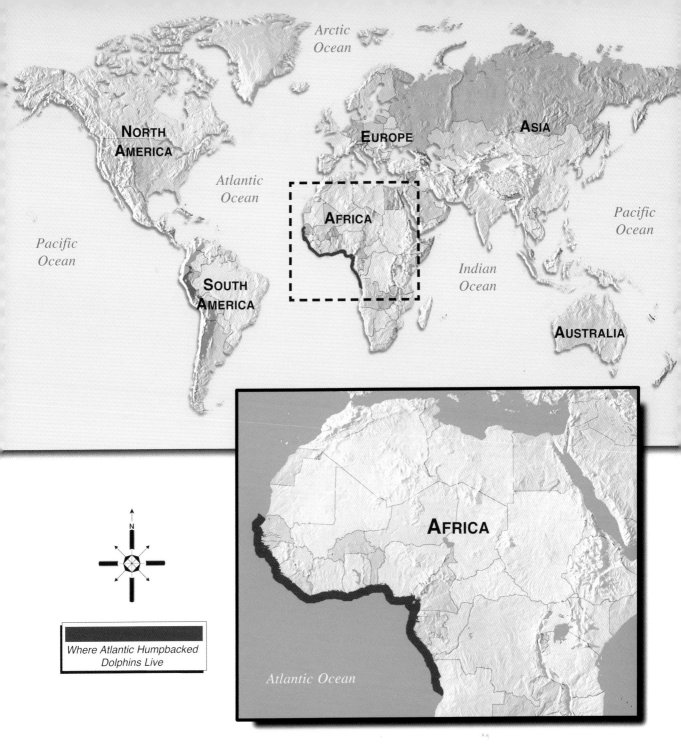

N

Where Atlantic Humpbacked
Dolphins Live

Arctic
Ocean

NORTH
AMERICA

EUROPE

ASIA

Atlantic
Ocean

AFRICA

Pacific
Ocean

Pacific
Ocean

SOUTH
AMERICA

Indian
Ocean

AUSTRALIA

AFRICA

Atlantic Ocean

Senses

Dolphins, whales, and some other mammals have a special sense that humans do not have. It is called echolocation. Dolphins use this sense to guide them

Dolphins also use sounds to communicate with each other.

through the water. If you had this ability, you could "see" without opening your eyes!

Echolocation is a complex and important process. First, dolphins make special noises. These noises travel through the surrounding water.

When the noise hits an object, it bounces off, or echoes. Then, the noise returns to the dolphin.

The dolphin uses this sound information to create a picture in its mind. Now, it can "see" what is around it and where it wants to go. Dolphins can also use this sense to escape from **predators**. And, they can use it to find their own prey.

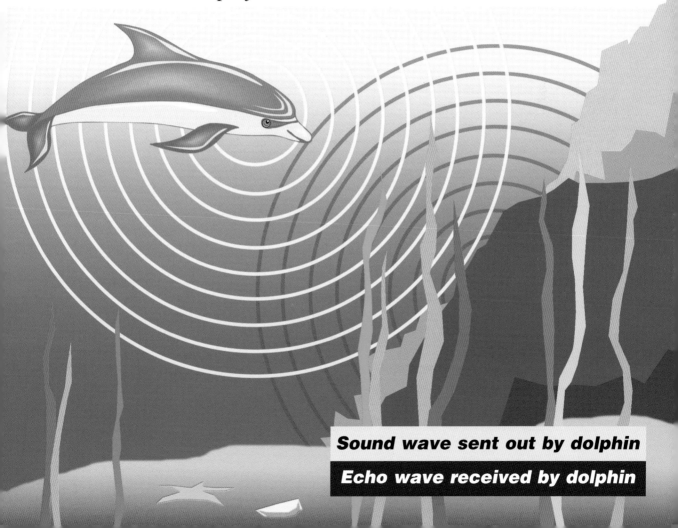

Sound wave sent out by dolphin

Echo wave received by dolphin

DEFENSE

Atlantic humpbacked dolphins face the same threats as many other dolphins. They are frequently caught in large fishing nets. Their waters may be polluted with chemicals from the land. They are sometimes hunted by humans. And, they are naturally hunted by killer whales.

Sometimes Atlantic humpbacks avoid predators by staying underwater for up to three minutes at a time. However, they usually surface every 40 to 60 seconds.

These dolphins have a good reason for staying close to land. Killer whales use echolocation to locate their prey. Land and other objects get in the way of this sense. This helps the dolphins remain hidden from their natural **predator**.

Killer whales eat a variety of foods.
They may eat anything from small
fish to large whales.

FOOD

Atlantic humpbacked dolphins use echolocation to find their prey. They eat small, schooling fish. They love herring, sea breams, mullet, and sardines. Other small

An Indo-Pacific humpbacked dolphin, such as this one, has 60 to 72 teeth. This helps scientists tell them apart from Atlantic humpbacked dolphins.

fish and **crustaceans** also make a tasty meal.

Atlantic humpbacked dolphins sometimes herd schools of fish toward land. These dolphins are likely to do this when feeding in small groups.

Moving their prey to shallow water makes these little fish easier to catch.

Many types of dolphins eat from schools of fish. Several dolphins will work together to get the school packed tight.

Atlantic humpbacked dolphins have about 26 to 31 pairs of teeth. These teeth are dull and look like pegs. The number and appearance of their teeth are important features. They help distinguish the Atlantic humpbacked dolphin from other similar dolphin species.

BABIES

Female Atlantic humpbacked dolphins are **pregnant** for 10 to 12 months. Baby dolphins are called calves. Typically, calves are born between December and February. However, these dolphins have been known to give birth during any month of the year.

Like other large mammals, usually one calf is born at a time. A mother dolphin nurses her calf with milk. Mother and calf stay together until the calf can feed on its own. Sometimes, calves stay for more than two years.

As adults, Atlantic humpbacked dolphins usually stay in **pods** of fewer than ten dolphins. However, they are often seen alone. Other times, Atlantic humpbacked dolphins are spotted in pods of 20 to 25 dolphins. These larger groups are usually made up of younger dolphins.

The Atlantic humpbacked dolphin's life span is unknown. But, some people estimate that they live at least 40 years.

BEHAVIORS

There is one important way Atlantic humpbacked dolphins interact with humans. The people of West Africa use this species in their fishing industry. When the dolphins and fishers work together, they both catch more fish!

These dolphins seem to have been trained for this job. Fishers signal them by hitting the water with sticks. When the dolphins hear this noise, they begin herding schools of fish. They eat fish on one side of the school. On the other side, fishers catch the fish in nets.

Atlantic humpbacked dolphins have other interesting behaviors. Some of them practice spyhopping. To do this, a dolphin peeks its head out of the water. Sometimes it spins around slowly as if scanning the area. Then, it dips back below the surface.

Humpbacked dolphins are slow swimmers. But, they are often more active when feeding and mating.

Young humpbacked dolphins love to lift their entire body out of the water. They like to **breach**, showing off their **dorsal** fin and back. Before the dolphin dives out of sight, it might pause. Or, it will simply flip its **flukes** as if waving goodbye.

ATLANTIC HUMPBACKED DOLPHIN FACTS

Scientific Name: *Sousa teuszii*

Common Names: Atlantic Humpbacked Dolphin, Cameroon Dolphin

Average Size: Adult Atlantic humpbacked dolphins are about 72 to 96 inches (183 to 244 cm) in length. They can weigh between 220 and 330 pounds (100 to 150 kg).

Where They're Found: Coastal waters off West Africa

Atlantic humpbacked dolphins are very similar to this Indo-Pacific humpbacked dolphin. But, people rarely confuse them because they live in different oceans!

GLOSSARY

breach - to jump or leap up out of the water.

cetacean (sih-TAY-shuhn) - any of various types of mammal, such as the dolphin, that live in the water like fish.

crustacean (kruhs-TAY-shuhn) - any of a group of animals with hard shells that live mostly in water. Crabs, lobsters, and shrimps are all crustaceans.

dorsal - located near or on the back, especially of an animal.

family - a group that scientists use to classify similar plants or animals. It ranks above a genus and below an order.

fluke - either of the fins that make up the tail of a cetacean, such as a whale or dolphin.

melon - the rounded forehead of some cetaceans, which may aid in echolocation.

migrate - to move from one place to another, often to find food.

pod - a group of animals, typically whales or dolphins.

predator - an animal that kills and eats other animals.

pregnant - having one or more babies growing within the body.

WEB SITES

To learn more about Atlantic humpbacked dolphins, visit ABDO Publishing Company on the World Wide Web at **www.abdopub.com**. Web sites about these dolphins are featured on our Book Links page. These links are routinely monitored and updated to provide the most current information available.

INDEX